LEARNING OF
DR. APJ ABDUL KALAM

An Impetus To The Youth

Ram Nivas Kumar
M.A. (English), MLISc., MJMC, Dip-in-OA

Copyright
Ram Nivas Kumar
First published August, 2018

Table of Contents

PREFACE

Dr. APJ Abdul Kalam was a world renowned scientist, the 11th President of India and an icon for the Indian youth and leaders. He was a true nationalist, legendary visionary and creative thinker. He was a great human being having excellence at par. He was the symbol of simplicity, wisdom and nationalism. He struggled hard throughout his life for the uplift of our country and development of nation.

After the sad demise of Dr. Kalam in July 2015, it cracked me all of a sudden that I must write a book in honour of Dr. APJ Abdul Kalam. Hence, I strived hard writing this book for years. While writing this book, I consulted several scholars, especially Dr. (Prof.) Arun Kumar 'Kamal', the Head of the Department of English, Patna University, Patna, for literary guidance. I also consulted Dr. (Prof.) Somnath Prasad, Ex-Head of the Department of English, Magadh University, Bodh Gaya, who helped me much writing this book. I went through several books by Dr. Kalam, the chief ones being "The Ignited Minds Unleashing The Power Within India", "Governance for Growth in India", "The Wings Of Fire", "India 2020", "My India: Ideas for the Future", "Turning Points: A Journey Through Challenges", "You Are Born To Blossom", "Forge Your Future", "Inspiring Thoughts", "Pathways to Greatness" and "Thoughts for Change: We Can Do It".

This book is a collection of his brilliant thoughts, innovative ideas and must-have learning on different topics. A large chapter with his brain storming quotes has been added at the end of the book. Lessons to the youth and the leaders of India have been included at large.

The learning of Dr. Kalam is meant for the people belonging to all strata of society of all religions and races. The book is useful particularly for the youth and the leaders of India. Hence, presentation of this book to the high hearts of Indian youth and leaders.

Its motto is to spread the learning of Dr. APJ Abdul Kalam. The youth and the leaders are requested to go through the book thoroughly. You will find bits of knowledge, pieces of information and points of learning to be learnt and adopted in the interest of the self and the nation.

While publishing this book, we have taken utmost care about the accuracy of the contents. We have strived hard to make the book errorless. However, to err is human. Inadvertent errors, if any, may please be brought to our notice. Comments and suggestions are most welcome.

Hope, the youth and the leaders would find this book as a treasure of nationalism and follow the advice of his highness Dr. APJ Abdul Kalam.

—Ram Nivas Kumar

CONTENTS

Leadership

Epilogue

1

INTRODUCTION

Dr. APJ Abdul Kalam was born on 15 October, 1931. His full name was Avul Pakir Jainulabddin Abdul Kalam. He was born in a Muslim family in Rameshwaram, then in Madras presidency in British India and now in the state of Tamil Nadu. His father Jainulabddin was a boat owner; his mother, Ashiamma, a housewife.

Dr. Kalam's ancestors were a happy family. But by the passage of time, the family lost most of its fortunes. His parents became poverty-stricken by the time Kalam was born. As a young boy, he had to sell newspapers in order to add to the family's meagre income.

He was a good student since his childhood. He was always curious to learn more about how things happened when he was ten years old. One of his teachers, Sir Subrahmania Iyer took the students to the seashore and asked them to observe the birds in flight. Then, the teacher gave the children a theoretical explanation coupled with the live practical example. It cast a deep influence on Kalam's mind. That very day, the boy realized that his life is calling for something to do with flight.

After completing his studies at Schwatz Higher Secondary School, he enrolled himself at Saint Joseph's College, Trichurapalli graduating in science in 1954. Pursuing his dream, he travelled to Madras to study aerospace engineering in Madras Institute of Technology.

During his third year, he was assigned a project to design a low-level attack aircraft together with a few other students. The project was a difficult one. Their guide gave him a very tight deadline. The young man toiled hard, worked under immense pressure and finally managed to achieve the target within the stipulated deadline. The teachers were thoroughly impressed by Kalam's dedication.

Dr. APJ Abdul Kalam is specialized in Aeronautical Engineering from Madras Institute of Technology. He is one of the most distinguished scientists of India and has received honorary doctorates from forty-five universities and institutions in India and abroad. He has been awarded the Padma Bhushan (1981), the Padma Vibhushan (1990) and India's highest civilian award, the Bharat Ratna (1997). He has also received the King Charles II Medal (2007), Woodrow Wilson Award (2008), the Hoover Award (2008) and the International Von Karman Wings Award (2009, among several other international accolades.

Dr. Kalam became the eleventh President of India on 25 July 2002. His greatest ambition is to find ways to transform India into a developed nation.

2

DR. KALAM AS A SCIENTIST

Dr. APJ Abdul Kalam earned his degree from Madras Institute of Technology in 1957 and joined the Aeronautical Development Establishment of the Defence Research and Development Organisation (DRDO) as a scientist in 1958.

In the early 1960, he worked with the Indian National Committee for Space Research under renowned space scientist Sir Vikram Sarabhai. He also designed a small hovercraft at DRDO. He worked on an expandable Docket Project independently at DRDO in 1965.

However, he was not much satisfied with his work at DRDO. He was happy to be transformed to the Indian Space Research Organisation in 1969. Then, he served as the Project Director of the SLV-III; the first indigenously designed and produced Satellite Launch Vehicle.

In 1970, he began making efforts to develop the Polar Satellite Launch Vehicle (PSLV) to allow India to launch its Indian Remote Sensing (IRS) Satellite into synchronous orbits. The nation's PSLV Project was eventually successful. It was first launched on 20 September, 1993.

Kalam also directed several other projects including projects development in the 1970s. Project Devil was an early liquid-fuelled missile project aimed at producing a shore-range Surface to Air Missile. The project was not a success in the long term and was discontinued in the 1980.

He was also involved with the project "Vallent" which aimed at the development of Intercontinental Ballistic Missile similar to project "Devil". This Project, too, was not a success in itself but played a role in the development of the Prithvi Missile later on.

In the early 1980, the Integrated Guided Missile Development Programme (IGMDP), Ministry of Defence programme, managed by the DRDO was launched. Kalam was asked to lead the project and thus he returned to DRDO as the Programme Chief Executive of the

IGMDP in 1983. It received tremendous political support. It aimed at the concurrent development of four projects- short range Surface to Surface Missile (Prithvi), short range Water to Surface to Air Missile (Trishul), medium range Surface to Air Missile (Akash) and third generation Anti-tank Missile (Nag).

The IGMDP, under the able leadership of Dr. Kalam, proved to be a resounding success. He further produced a number of successful missiles including the first Prithvi missile in 1989. Due to his achievements as the Director of the IGMDP, APJ Abdul Kalam earned the nickname of "Missile Man." His increasing involvement with government agencies led to his appointment on the scientific administrator to the Defence Minister in 1992.

In 1999, he was appointed as the Principal Scientific Advisor to the Government of India in the rank of Cabinet Minister.

In the late 1990, he played a major role in conducting the Pokhran-II, a series of five nuclear bomb test explosions, at the Indian Army's Pokhran Test Range in May, 1998. Following the success of these tests which elevated Dr. Kalam to the status of a national hero, the then Prime Minister Atal Bihari Vajpai declared India a full-fledged nuclear State.

In addition to being a brilliant scientist, APJ Abdul Kalam was also a big visionary. In 1998, he proposed a country wide plan called Technology Vision, 2020 to serve as an action plan to make India a developed nation by the year, 2020. He put forward several suggestions including nuclear power technological innovations, and improved agriculture production to achieve.

3

DR. KALAM AS THE PRESIDENT OF INDIA

In 2002, the National Democratic Alliance (NDA), which was in power, expressed its decision to nominate APJ Abdul Kalam for the President of India to succeed outgoing President Dr. K.R. Narayanan. Dr. Kalam being a popular figure easily won the presidential election.

Dr. APJ Abdul Kalam assumed the Office of the 11th President of India on 25 July, 2002. He became the first scientist to occupy Rashtrapati Bhavan. Over the work of his five-year term, he remained committed to his vision of transforming India into a developed nation and thus spent a lot of time on conducting meetings with young people to inspire them to achieve their best.

He proved to be very popular with the citizens of the country and became known as the people's President. He was, however, criticized for not taking any concrete actions on the mercy petitions of court cases on death row submitted to him during his tenure. Out of the 21 mercy petitions submitted to him, he acted on only one plea in his five-year tenure.

In 2007, he decided not to contest the presidential election again and stepped down as the President on 25July, 2007.

POST PRESIDENCY

Dr. APJ Abdul Kalam ventured into the academic field after leaving the Office. He became a visiting Professor at several reputed institutions including the Indian Institute of Management, Shillong; the Institute of Management, Ahmadabad; and the Indian Institute of Management, Indore. He interacted with bright young minds at large length which developed as his passion in the later years.

The post presidency years also saw him teaching Information Technology at the International Institute of Information Technology, Hyderabad; the Institute of Technology at Banaras Hindu University and Anna University. He also served as the Chancellor of the Indian Institute of Space Science and Technology at Thiruvananthapuram.

In 2012, he launched a programme called "giving attitude" for the youth and to encourage them to contribute towards nation building by taking small but positive steps.

AFTERWARDS AND ACHIEVEMENTS

Kalam was the proud recipient of Padma Bhushan, Padma Vibhushan and Bharat Ratna Awards from Government of India. He received these awards in the year 1981, 1990 and 1997 respectively.

In 1997, he was honoured by the Government of India with Indira Gandhi Award for National Integration. Later, the next year, he was awarded the Veer Savarkar Award by the Government of India.

The Alwar Research Centre, Chennai bestowed Kalam with Ramanujan Awards in the year 2000. Dr. Kalam was honoured with the King Charles's Medal by the Royal Society, UK in 2007. In 2008, he received the Hoover Award given by ASMD Foundation, USA. The California Institute of Technology, USA presented Dr. Kalam with the International Von Karman Wings Award in the year 2009. Dr. Kalam was the proud recipient of honorary doctorates from 45 universities of India and abroad. In addition, his birthday was recognised as World Students Day by United Nations.

PERSONAL LIFE AND LEGACY

APJ Abdul Kalam was the younger child in a close knit family. He was very close to his parents, especially his mother, and had loving relationship with all of his four elder brothers.

He never maintained himself throughout his life. He maintained close ties with his brothers and their extended families. A benevolent soul, he often sent money to his elderly relatives.

He was a very simple person who led an unpretentious lifestyle. He owned a few possessions including his beloved veena and collections of books. He could not even have a television. A kind hearted man, he was a vegetarian and consumed simple food.

A devout Muslim, he raised with strict Islam customs. He respected all religions. He was well versed in Hindu traditions in addition to his

Islamic practices. He not only read the Namaz daily and fasted during Ramadan, but also regularly read the Bhagavada Gita.

He remained active till the very end. While delivering a lecture at the Indian Institute of Management, Shillong on 27 July, 2015, he collapsed and was rushed to the Bethany Hospital where he was confirmed dead of cardiac arrest at 7.45 am. The Government of India declared seven-days State mourning as a mark of respect.

4

LEARNING OF DR. KALAM

Following is the pieces of learning of Dr. APJ Abdul Kalam collected from his different books to be read and followed by every youth and politician of our country:

Dr. Kalam says: Spirituality must be integrated with education. Self-realization is the focus. Each of us must become aware of our higher Self. We are links of a great past to a grand future. We should ignite over dormant inner energy and let it guide our lives. The radiance of such minds embarked on constructive endeavour will bring peace, prosperity and bliss to this nation.

Dream, dream, dream;

Dreams transform into thoughts;

And thoughts result in action.

Men often become what they believe themselves to be. If I believe—I cannot do anything, it makes me incapable of doing. But when I believe—I can, I acquire the ability to do even if I did not have it in the beginning.

A nation's wealth is the young generation of the country. When they grow up, they can be the role models. Mother, father and elementary school teachers play a very important part of role models. When the child grows up, the role models will be national leaders of quality and integrity in every field including politics, science, technology and industry.

Whatever you can—just do or dream. You can begin it. Boldness has genius. It has power. It has magic in it. Begin it just now.

The great minds of the country have the ability to make others convert dreams into reality. For them, the nation is bigger than themselves. They could draw thousands to act upon their dreams.

The fundamental thing you must know is that he who deserves the good things of life, the benefits God bestows. Unless our students and the youth believe that they are worthy of being citizens of a developed India, how will they ever be responsible and enlightened citizens?

There is nothing mysterious about the abundance in developed nation. The historic fact is that the people of these nations—the G8, as they are called, believed over many generations that they must live a good life in a strong and prosperous nation. The reality becomes aligned with their aspirations.

I do not think that abundance and spirituality are mutually exclusive. I do not believe that it is wrong to desire material thing. For instance, while I personally cherish a life with minimum of possessions, I admire abundance for it brings along with it security and confidence. These eventually help preserve our freedom. Nature, too, does not do anything by half measures, as you will see if you look around you. Go to a garden. In season, there is a profusion of flowers. Look them up. The universe stretches into infinite; vast beyond belief.

All that we see in the world is an embodiment of energy. We are a part of the cosmic energy, too. Therefore, when we begin to appreciate that spirit and matter are both parts of existence, they are in harmony with each other. We shall realize that it is wrong to feel that it is somehow shameful or non-spiritual to desire material things. If parents and teachers show the required dedication to shape the lives of the young, India would get a new life.

Behind the parents stands the school, and behind the teacher stands the home. Education and the teacher-student relationship have to be seen not in business terms but with the nation's growth in mind. A proper education would help nurture a sense of dignity and self-respect. These are the qualities no law can enforce- they have to be nurtured themselves.

It seems to me that both—good and evil will survive side by side. The Almighty does help them both. "How to minimize the evil through our spiritual growth" is a question that has persisted throughout human history.

If there are no dreams, there are no revolutionary thoughts. If there are no thoughts, no actions will emanate. Hence, parents and teachers should allow their children to dream. Success always follows dreams. Though, there may be some setbacks and delays.

Visionary action is needed when you grow up. You will probably be a part of reconstructing this nation and giving shape to these thoughts. Agni symbolizes our strength. It shows that India has all the capabilities.

Role models can help us focus on what is correct for us as individuals, as groups, and, of course, as a nation. They can also lead us to great success. We seem to have got carried away with the success of a few in the field of information technology.

There is a unique characteristic of our country to belittle our capabilities. It may even be genetic. I say: India can design, develop and produce any type of missile and any type of nuclear weapon. This is a capability only four countries in the world have. Remove all the doubts from your mind.

Ancient India was a knowledge society. It was a leader in many intellectuals, media and astronomy. A renaissance is imperative for us to once again become a knowledge superpower than simply providing cheap labour in areas of high technology.

Diseases normally require intensive treatment. But even the medicine acknowledges that our minds can play a major role.

Vision ignites the mind. India needs visionaries of the stature of JRD Tata, Vikram Sarabhai, Satish Dhawan and Dr. Verghese Kurien, to name a few, who can involve an entire generation in mission drive programmes which benefit the country as a whole.

5

LEARNING FROM SAINTS AND SEERS

Following is the learning of different Indians saints and seers that we must read and follow:

For the society to prosper, there are two important needs. They are prosperity through wealth generation and cherishing the value system of the people. The combination of the two will make the nation truly strong and prosperous.

Dr. Kalam always tells the young to dream. This message comes from the understanding that each one of us has within ourselves the ability to create the circumstances for success. We have the ability to act what we desire.

We can easily say that there is a magnetic field at work that we cannot detect it with our senses even though it is everywhere on our planet. Logically then, it is in us also.

Similarly, our planet is in a perpetual state of motion as it goes spinning through space. Everything on the planet is a part of this movement, even though it appears to us that we are motionless. We are on the planet. And thus, we are a part of the energy that moves it. The energy that is the essence of the planet is in us.

The unification of science and spirituality will be essential to take the benefit of science and technology to mankind.

We have learnt over the years to maintain our equanimity regardless of circumstances. We have faced failures and disappointments without feeling defeated. We wish to live the rest of my life at peace with ourselves and others. We have no wish to engage in quarrels with others.

There is always the challenge before an individual as he tries to transcend his limitations.

What we are and what we believe in are in ours alone. Hence, we have trust in wisdom that created us. We can develop a faith that sustains us through our lives.

Indians are well versed with the concept of higher Self, or perhaps highest Self is the preferable term. For generations, our ancestors lived their lives by this concept. But for many today, rooted perhaps too deeply in the material world, this idea sounds lofty and spiritual. For us, it has been a cornerstone of the way we live.

Dr. Kalam here gives us three nuggets of wisdom:

1. "When you speak, speak the truth; perform when you promise. Withhold your hands from striking and from taking which is unlawful and bad."
2. "What actions are most excellent to gladden the heart of a human being, to feed the hungry, to help the afflicted, to lighten the sorrow of the sorrowful and to remove the wound of the injured."
3. "All God's creatures are His family; and he is the most beloved of God who tries to do most good to God's creatures."

Let us remember the Rig Veda: 'Aano Bhadrah Kratavo Yenthu Yishwathaha.' That is, 'Let noble thoughts come to us from every side.'

Our spiritual wisdom has been our strength. We as a nation survived the onslaughts of invaders and the numbing effects of colonialism. We have also learnt to adjust to the rifts and divisions in our own society. But in the process of all the adjustment, we have lowered our aims and expectations. We must regain our broad outlook and draw upon our heritage and wisdom to enrich our lives. The fact that we advance technologically does not preclude spiritual development. We need to home-grow our own model of development based on our inherent strengths.

6

POSITIVE THINKING

There is a law in Psychology that if you form a picture in your mind of what you would like to be, and you keep and hold that picture there long enough, you will soon become exactly as you have been thinking.

—William James

If you paint in your mind a picture of bright and happy expectations, you put yourself into a condition conducive to your goals. —Norman Vincent Peale

The way you think and feel about yourself, including your belief and expectation about what is possible for you, determines everything you do and everything that happens to you.

You have complete control over only one thing in the universe- your thinking. You can decide what you are going to think in any given situation. Your thoughts and the way you interpret any event trigger your feelings- positive or negative. Your thoughts and feelings lead to your actions and determine the result you get. It all starts with your thoughts.

Positive thoughts are life changing. They empower you and make you feel stronger and more confident. Positive thinking is not just a motivational idea. It has measurable, constructive effects on your personality, your heath, your level of energy, and your creativity. The more positive and optimistic you are, the happier you will be in every area of your life.

Negative thoughts bring about the opposite. They disempower you and make you feel weaker and less confident. Whenever you think and say something negative, you give your power away. You feel angry and defensive. You feel frustrated and unhappy. Over time, negative thinking can make you physically ill, and even poison your relationships.

Positive thinking leads to mental health, peace and good performance. Negative thinking leads to mental illness and deceased effectiveness. Your goal, therefore, if you want to live a wonderful life, is to cultivate positive emotions and get rid of negative emotions.

The eliminating of negative emotions is the most important single step you can take towards health, happiness, and personal well-being. Each time you take complete control over thoughts and feelings, and discipline yourself to keep them positive, the quality of both—your inner and outer lives improves. In the absence of negative emotions, your mind automatically fills with the positive emotions that generate feelings of happiness and fulfilment.

7

CHOOSE YOUR THOUGHTS

The Law of Substitution says, "Your mind can hold only one thought at a time—positive or negative. You can substitute a positive thought for a negative one whenever you choose." You can apply this law by deliberately thinking about something positive whenever you want to cancel out a thought or feeling that makes you angry or unhappy.

The Law of Habit says, "Any thought or action that you repeat over and over will eventually become a new habit. When you repeatedly react and respond in a positive way, you take full control over your conscious mind. Soon it becomes automatic and easy to think and act in that manner. By using will power and repetition, you develop new habits of thinking and acting. By applying this law, you can become a completely positive person and change your life."

STARVE NEGATIVE EMOTION

Many negative ideas and attitudes are based on false premises. Sometimes a negative idea about a subject or a negative attitude toward a person can be completely reversed with a single piece of new information. You could suddenly learn that an idea you had about yourself or another person was not true. As a result, you could change your thinking in an instant.

Negative emotion exists because we give them life and keep them alive. We feel them by continually thinking and talking about things that make us angry or unhappy. Fortunately, you can choose this situation by applying the Law of Emotion. This law states, "A stronger emotion will dominate and override a weaker emotion, and whichever motion you concentrate becomes stronger."

This means that whatever emotion you dwells upon grows and eventually dominates your thinking in that area. If you withdraw your mental energy from a person or situation that makes you sad or angry by refusing to think about it, the emotion connected with that situation eventually dies away. Like a fire, with no fuel, it goes out.

STOP JUSTIFYING

Justification is what you do when you rationalize or crate a reason for your anger and unhappiness. You tell yourself—how badly you were treated and how dreadfully the other person behaved. You continue rehearse the situation in your mind. You repeat all the reasons you have for being upset. Each time you think of the person or situation, you become angry.

You should stop justifying your negative emotions. Remember, your negative emotions do you no good. They are totally destructive. They do not affect the other person or change the situation. They simply undermine your happiness and self-confidence. They make you weaker and less effective in other areas of your life. Instead of justifying your anger and unhappiness, you should use your intelligence to let go the unhappy situation.

INTERPRET EVENTS DIFFERENTLY

The author and speaker Wayne Dyer says, "It is never too late to have a happy childhood." He means that at any time you can interpret the unhappy events of your early life in a positive way. You should look into those negative experiences for something good and think about that instead. You can focus on how your unhappy experiences have made you a better, wiser person. You can be grateful to people who have hurt you in the past because they have made you so much stronger in the present.

DREAM BIG DREAMS

Dream lofty dreams, and as you dream, so shall you become. Your vision is the promise you shall at last unveil. —John Ruskin

Your mind can be your best friend or your worst enemy. Your thoughts alone have the power to make you healthy or sick, rich or poor, popular or unpopular. Your mind is like powerful forces that can be tuned in any direction to bring about wonderful results or havoc and destruction. Your main goal in life must be to harness your amazing powers and direct them intelligently and systematically toward achieving everything you really want.

Your aim is to become so confident, courageous, strong and resolute that you can get any goal with the firm knowledge that you can learn what you need to learn, and you can do what you need to do. You will become so persistent and determined that nothing and no one can slow you down or alter your course.

By the Law of Correspondence, whatever you can clearly see the inside, you will eventually experience on the outside. You should, therefore, visualize your goals with as much clarity and vividness as possible. You should visualize your goals intensely and you should create within yourself the same feeling that you would have if you had already achieved your goals. Visualize your goals frequently. Replay a picture of your goal, as if you had already realized it, on the screen of your mind as many times a day as you possibly can. Visualize your goals for as long as you possibly can, preferably just before falling asleep each night.

8

CREATE YOUR IDEAL LIFE STYLE

The most important part of dreaming big dreams for you is to define your ideal future vision. It is for you to think about what you want before you begin to think about what is possible for you. You dream big dreams by looking into the future and imagine that you have no limitations holding you from achieving anything you set your mind on.

Detach yourself from your current situation and allow yourself to dream. Pretend for the moment that you have all the time and money you need. Imagine that you have all the connections and contacts, all the resources and opportunities, all the education and knowledge, all the skill and experience that you require to be, have, or do anything that you could dream of.

Imagine your ideal lifestyle. Imagine your ideal job or income. Imagine where you would like to live and how you would like to spend each day, each week, each month. Imagine your ideal family life. Imagine your ideal state of health. Design your perfect life in every respect.

DECIDE EXACTLY WHAT YOU WANT

A real goal is clear, specific, measurable, and time bound. A wish or a hope is fuzzy and unclear. It is fantasy that floats in the air. People with clear and specific goal, who know exactly what they want, are very different from the people who are going through life hoping for the best. Your ability to decide exactly what you want in each area of your life is one of the most important responsibilities of your life.

One of the major reasons that people fail in life is because they waste so much of their time doing things of low value or no value at all. And the reason they waste so much time is because they have no real idea of what they really want. Once you have clear goal, your ability to manage your time improves dramatically.

To realize your full potential, your greatest need is to break out of your limited thinking by aiming big dreams and imaging unlimited possibilities. You need to remove all the negative beliefs that hold you back from becoming capable of everything.

WRITE DOWN YOUR GOALS

Write your goals down on paper. There is something quite incredible that happens between the brain and the hand. When you take a paper or a pen and write down your goals, you intensify your belief and deepen your conviction that your goals are possible for you. The very act of writing down your goals gives you a sense of central and personal power. Written goals increase your resolve and determination to do whatever is necessary to achieve them.

MAKE A DETAILED PLAN

Make a plan in writing. Remember, the ability to develop written goals and create plans for their achievement is a matter of skill of success. A plan begins with making a list of the entire things that you do to achieve your goal. Once you have made your list, you can add new items as they occur to you.

A plan of action gives you a tract to run on. It increases your sense of belief. It intensifies your desire for the goal. You gradually become convinced that your goal is actually possible and achievable by you.

TAKE ACTION ON YOUR PLAN

Take action of some kind in the direction of your goal. Once you have set a goal, written it down, determined the price that you are going to have to pay, and made a plan, you must take some action immediately. Even if you only make a phone call or collect a piece of information, be sure to do something. In the Bible it says, "Faith without deeds is dead."

There is something powerful in your willingness to take a specific action. Your action itself seems to trigger all kinds of powers and forces in the universe. When you take action, you demonstrate to yourself and to others for that matter, that you are really serious about your goal.

Until you have taken a specific, irrevocable action of some kind, you have merely engaged in an enjoyable exercise like day dreaming. You have put your key into the ignition but you haven't turned it on.

DO SOMETHING EVERYDAY

Do something every day that moves you towards your most important goal. This is vital principle that generates energy and enthusiasm. For you, to maintain your courage, confidence, and self-motivation, you must be doing something every single day that gives you a feeling of forward motion and progress. Your job is to build yourself up to the point where you genuinely feel unstoppable. The only way that you can do this is by refusing to stop, by doing something daily.

NEVER GIVE UP

Resolve in advance that you will never quit, once you have started towards you goal. No matter how many setbacks or obstacles you experience. Make the decision that you will help on pleasing yourself up. Make the decision that you will persist until you fully succeed. When the difficulties arise, you will be mentally prepared to plough through them rather than quitting. Your willingness and ability to persist are what will eventually guarantee your success.

ACTION EXCERCISES

You are an earnest. Seek this minutely whatever you can do or dream. Boldness has genius, power, and magic in it. You only engage and the mind grows heated. Begin with your work and the task will be completed. Following is the key exercises for you:

- What one great goal would you set for yourself?
- Make out a "dream list." Write down everything you would like to have in your life someday.
- Imagine your perfect life style, if you were financially independent and you could live anyway and anywhere you wanted, what would you change?
- Make a list of ten goals you would like to accomplish in the next year. From that list, select one goal that would have the greatest positive impact on your life if you could achieve it right now.
- Write your most important goal on a separate piece of paper. Make it measurable and set a deadline for its accomplishment.
- Make a written plan to achieve this goal. Write out a list of everything you can think of. You will have to do to accomplish it.
- Take action on your plan immediately that moves you towards that goal. Never miss a day until you have achieved it.

THINK LIKE A GENIUS

Make every thought that comes into your mind pay you a profit. Make it work and produce with you. Think of things not as they are but as they might be. Don't merely dream but create. —Maxwell Maltz

You are a potential genius. The number of possible thoughts you can think is greater than all the molecules known in the universe. You have the capacity to learn at incredible rates and to retain more information than you can even imagine. It is said, "When an educated person dies, it is as if a library is burnt down."

KNOWLEDGE IS A GREAT RESOURCE

Today the primary source of value is knowledge, since there is no limit to the amount of knowledge you can acquire. There is no limit to the amount of value that you can create. You can start from wherever you are, no matter what your background is. You can start your work today on improving your ability to perform and get results for which others will pay.

The wonderful thing about knowledge is that it can be reproduced hundreds of thousands or even millions of times without tossing its value. It is the one commodity that can actually be infinite in its application. If you or someone else comes up with a new idea to do something faster or better, that idea can be spread around the world in no time at all. That idea can be in the hands of millions of other people who can also use it to improve their lives. And you lose nothing.

SMALL DIFFERENCES LEAD TO BIG RESULTS

Often small improvements in the way you think and perform can lead to significant improvements in your performance. It is not necessary for you to attend university and get years of education to bring your knowledge up to the level where it can pay off for you. Sometimes very small changes in what you are doing can give amazing results.

UNLEASH YOUR MENTAL POWERS

The potential of the average person is like a huge ocean unsailed; a new continent unexplored, a world of possibilities waiting to be released and channelled towards some great good.

—Brian Tracy

Every change in your life will come about as the result of your mind colliding with a new idea. Ideas are the keys to the future. Ideas contain answers to all of your problems. They contain the ways to achieve your goals. Your need is to become an idea generator so that you are continually coming up with new and better ideas to deal with the continuous changes and opportunities taking place around you.

Fortunately, you are naturally creative. It is an innate quality. You are born with it. But creativity is subject to the Law of Use which says, "If you don't use it, you lose it; at least temporarily." The good news is that you can reignite your creativity by practicing the specific.

THREE MINDS IN ONE

You think and operate your life with three different minds:

1. The first is your conscious mind. You use your conscious mind to take in new information, compare it with your current knowledge, analyse it in terms of its value or relevance to you and then decide to act or not to act. This is the mind with which you direct your life. This is often referred to as the objective mind.

2. The second mind you use is your subconscious. Your subconscious mind is a huge data bank that records every thought, idea, emotion, or experience that you ever have throughout your life. This is called the subjective mind. Its role is to keep all of your words and actions consistent with your current attitudes, beliefs, fears, and prejudices. Your subconscious mind does not reason; it only obeys your commands.

Your subconscious mind is also responsible for the operation of all of your bodily functions. It controls your nervous system and your heart rate. It controls your breathing, digestion, basic memory and so on. It is like a huge computer so powerful and precise that it can process a hundred million commands per second.

1. Your third mind is your super conscious mind. This mind is your direct connection with infinite intelligence. It contains all knowledge. It can bring you all the ideas and answers you will ever need to achieve. This mind is the source of all inspiration, imagination and intuition. It is stimulated by clear goals, vivid mental pictures, and positive commands in the form of affirmations.

When you use all three minds in harmony with each mind performing the functions for which it was designed, you will accomplish more of your goals faster than you have ever imagined.

THINKING AHEAD

If you are a normal intelligent person, you will organize each area of your life to avoid failure and disappointment as much as possible. You will think ahead and anticipate what could go wrong. You will then take necessary precautions to award against setbacks and problems.

Disappointment comes in spite of your best efforts to avoid it. It is inevitable and unavoidable. As the sun rises in the east and sets in the west, you are going to experience disappointments in life. The more goals you set and the more things you try, the more difficulties and problems you will have.

Successful people respond to disappointment differently from unsuccessful people. The way you deal with disappointment is an extremely good predictor of whatever you will achieve in your field or in life overall.

Since you cannot always avoid disappointment, no matter what you do. The only thing that matters is how you deal with the disappointment when it comes upon you unwanted and unexpected. Successful people deal with disappointment by taking it in stride. Unsuccessful people allow disappointment to continue. Successful people recover and continue forward. Unsuccessful people often quit and go back. Motivational speaker Charlie Jones says, "It is not how far you fall, but how high you bounce that counts."

LIVE A GREAT LIFE

The only true measure of success is the ratio between what we might have done and what we might have been to the one hand, and the things we have done and the things we have made of ourselves on the other. —H. G. Wells

The Law of Correspondence is perhaps the most important of all laws in determining your success or failure in life. The law says that your outer world is a reflection of your inner world. It says that whatever you are on the inside, you will soon see the results of it in the outside. When you change your thinking, you change your life.

The law applies to everything you do. Your inner world of knowledge and preparation will determine your outer world. Your inner world of personality development will determine your outer world of friendships and relationships. Your inner attitude of health and fitness will determine the condition of your physical body. Your inner beliefs and expectations will determine your outer attitudes and your behaviour towards other people. Your outer world will always reflect your inner world.

HAPPINESS IS THE SUPREME GOAL

Aristotle, perhaps the greatest of the philosophers, wrote more than 2300 years ago that the ultimate aim of all human action is happiness. He concluded that everything a person does is to achieve happiness of some kind. Sometimes they are successful and sometimes they are unsuccessful, but happiness is always the target each person aims at.

He concluded that every act is merely an interim step in the direction of happiness. For example, you want to get a good job. Why? So you can earn good money. Why? So you can get a comfortable home and a nice car. Why? So you can have good relationships and a nice family. Why? So you can have a satisfying home life. Why? The final action, the ultimate goal, is so that you can be happy. Everything that anyone else does is aimed at happiness.

THE ROLE OF GOODNESS

One of Aristotle's greatest insights on the subject of happiness is his conclusion that only the good can be happy, and only the virtuous can be good. This is one of the most important observations in the history of human thought and experience. Only the good can be happy, and only the virtuous can be good.

LIVE WITHIN YOUR INCOME

Your ability to save money and to discipline yourself to live within your income is a key measure of your ability to succeed in life. If you do not have the internal self-control to refrain from spending everything you earn, this suggests that you probably do not have the discipline necessary to succeed in other areas of your life. Although the Bible says that the love of money is the root of all evils, it is far more likely that the lack of money is the root of all evils.

Perhaps the greatest benefit of saving our money and building up a cash reserve is that it enables you to take advantages of opportunities when they arise.

INTEGRITY IS ESSENTIAL

The most important single quality for success is your integrity. Aristotle insisted that only a life based on value such as integrity, honesty, courage, generosity, persistence and sincerity would lead to happiness and personal fulfilment. Once you have determined your values, your level of integrity can be measured by how rigidly you adhere to them. A value is not something that you compromise when it is convenient.

SUMMARY AND CONCLUSIONS

The world is like a great mirror. It reflects back to you what you are. If you love it, you are friendly. If you are helpful, the world will prove loving, friendly, and helpful to you. The world is what you are. —Thomas Dreier

The most important principle of human life is that you become what you think about most of the time. This insight is the foundation of religion, philosophy, metaphysics, psychology, and all success. Your outer world is very much a reflection of your inner world. If you change your thinking, you change your life.

Your biggest challenge and your greatest responsibility are to create within yourself the mental equivalent of what you want to experience on the outside. By doing this, you activate all your mental powers and put the forces of the universe to work on your behalf. You take full control over your life.

9

STEPS TO HIGH PERFORMANCE LIVING

Forget your own unhappiness by creating little happiness for others because when you are good to others, you are best to yourself. Just remember—the things you do for yourself are gone when you are gone, but the things you do for others remain as your legacy.

In addition to looking for the good and seeking the valuable lesson, optimists have seven orientations and generalized ways of thinking about themselves and their lives. There are the seven subjects that they think about most of the time:

1. Think About The Future

First, happy people are future oriented. They think and talk about the future much of the time. They think and talk about where they are going rather than about what has happened in the past. They create a clear, exiting future vision of what is possible for them. By the Law of Attraction, they find themselves attracted towards their further hopes and dreams. And their future hopes and dreams are attracted towards them.

1. Think About Your Goals

Second, they are goal oriented. They think and talk about their goals much of the time. Once they have dreamed and fantasized about their ideal future vision, they boil them down into clear, written goals and plans that they work on every day. They focus their attention and concentrate their energies. They use their goals to take control over their futures.

1. Think About Excellence

Third, they are excellence oriented. They commit to becoming excellent at what they do to joining the top ten per cent of people in their field. They identify their key result areas and set standard of excellent performance for themselves in each area. They work on themselves each day, and never stop improving.

1. Think About The Solution

Fourth, they are solution-oriented. They think about the solution rather than the problem. They think about things to be done rather than who is to blame. They use creativity and that of the people around them. They see their problems to be solved. They believe that there is a logical solution to every difficulty.

1. Think About The Result

Fifth, successful and happy people are intensely result-oriented. They carefully plan each day in advance. They set clear priorities on their activities. They then work on those tasks that represent the most valuable use of their time. They plough through numerous amounts of work and become known a highly productive people because they are so effective and efficient, they get more done. They move ahead faster, and they make a greater contribution to their work and to their world.

1. Think About High Performance

Sixth, high performance is growth oriented. They are continually reading, listening to audio programs, and attending additional courses and seminars. They are determined to stay at the cutting edge of their fields. They know that the future belongs to the competent. It belongs to those few people who know more than their competitions. They know that there is a race on, and that they are in it. They are determined to win.

1. Think About Action

Seventh and perhaps more important than any of the others, the most successful people are intensely action-oriented. They think about what they can do right now to move faster towards their goals. They are in constant motion. They work in real time. They have a sense of urgency. They cover more ground and get a lot more done than the average person. The more they get done, the better they get. The more value they get, the more they earn.

10

CORE IDEAS FOR THE YOUTH

We are living in the golden age of mankind. There have never been more opportunities and possibilities for you to become capable of doing, and to achieve more of your goals than they are today. You can use this book as a guide to great success and happiness for the rest of your life. Here are the core ideas:

1. **Change Your Thinking:** The way you think about yourself, your abilities, your potential and your self-concept determines everything you are today, and everything you ever will be. Fortunately, your self-concept is learned. By taking complete control over different things, pictures, and ideas let into your mind, you take complete control of your future.

1. **Change Your Life:** You come into the world as pure potential with unlimited abilities in countless areas. As a result of destructive criticism in childhood, you can inadvertently develop fears of failure, rejection and criticism. You can develop self-limiting beliefs that hold you back. By getting rid of these negative emotions, you liberate your potential and change your life.

1. **Dream Some Dreams:** The true starting point of living the kind of life that is possible for you is to create an exciting future vision of what you would want your life to be in every area, if you had no limitations at all. Imagine that you could be, have, or do anything at all in your family, finances, and personal life. Then set clear, written goals, backed by detailed plane to make your dreams come true.

1. **Decide To Become Rich:** Resolve today to make complete control over your financial future. Begin to do the things that

others have done to become financially independent starting from where you are today. Determine exactly how much you want to earn, keep, and acquire. Set these amounts in goals and then think about them all the time. Whatever others have done, you can do as well.

1. **Accept Challenge In Your Life:** You are the primary creative force in your own life. Everything you are or ever will be will be the result of what you do or fail to do. Resolve today to accept hundred per cent responsibility with no beaming and no excuses for anything that happens. Exert your personal power and take control of your thoughts, words, and actions. Be the master of your own destiny.

1. **Commit To Excellence:** The biggest reward and the greatest satisfaction go to those who are very good at what they do. Resolve to join the top ten per cent of people in your field. Defer more the skills you will have to excel at what you do. Set superior performance as your goal, make a plan, and then work on getting better every day.

1. **Put People First:** The quality and quantity of your relationships will have more of an impact on your success and happiness than any other tutors. Organize your life around maintaining high quality, high trust relationships with the most important people in your world network. Regularly work to expand your range of contacts. Master it with other positive and success-oriented people.

1. **Mental Fitness And Physical Fitness:** It takes a long time and a lot of hard work to achieve it and maintain it. But it is worth every bit of efforts you put in. The payoff can be extraordinary.

When you begin the process of working on yourself to create on the inside a clear picture of what you want to enjoy on the outside, process may be slow at first. But when you persist, when you keep doing and saying the right thing in the right way, you will, before too long, set results out of all preparation to the effort you put it.

11
PATRIOTISM BEHIND POLITICS

"I do not care for liberation. I would rather go to a hundred thousand hells, 'doing good to others (silently) like the spring', -this is my religion." —Swami Vivekananda

Walking is an essential part of one's life. Wherever Dr. Kalam went, he made it a point to walk five kilometres in the morning. He told us to be particularly attached to seeing the beauty of the sunrise. Enjoy the birds that sing to welcome the dawning of a new day on this planet.

I call to my people to rise to greatness. It is a call to all Indians to rise to their highest capabilities. What are the forces which lead to the rise or fall of nations? And what are the factors which go to make a nation strong? These factors are invariably found in a strong nation- a collective pride in its achievements, unity and the ability for combined action. All nations which have risen to greatness have been characterised by a sense of mission.

The greatest danger to our sense of unity and our sense of purpose comes from those ideologies who seek to divide the people. The Indian constitution bestows on all the citizens total equality under its protective umbrella. What is now concern is the trend towards putting religious form over religious sentiments. Why can't we develop a cultural—not religious—context for our heritage that serves to make Indians of us all? The time has come for us to stop differentiation. What we need today is a vision to the nation which can bring unity.

It is when we accept India in all its splendid glory that, with a shared past as a base, we can look forward to a shared future of peace and prosperity, of creation and abundance. Our past is there with us forever. It has to be nurtured in good faith. It is not to be destroyed in exercise of political one-upmanship.

The developed India will not be a nation of cities. It will be a network of prosperous villages. It will be empowered by telemedicine, tele-education, and e-commerce. The new India will emerge out of the combination of bio-technology, bio-science and agriculture science and industrial development. The political leaders would be working with the zeal born of the knowledge that a nation is bigger than individual interests and political parties.

The most important and urgent task before our leadership is to get all the forces for constructive change together and deploy them in a mission mode. India is a country of one billion people with numerous religions and communities. It offers wide spectrum of ideologies, besides its geographic diversity. This is our greatest strength. However, fragmented thinking, compartmentalized planning and isolated efforts are not yielding results. The people have to come together to create a harmonious India.

The second vision of the nation will bring about renaissance to the nation. The task of casting a strong India is in the hands of a visionary political leadership.

There are success stories among failures. There is hope among chaos. There is promise among problems. We are one billion people with multiple faiths and ideologies. In the absence of a national vision, cracks at the seam keep surfacing and make us vulnerable. There is a need to reinforce this seam and amalgamate us into one national freedom.

12

THE KNOWLEDGE SOCIETY

Wisdom is a weapon to ward off destruction. It is an inner fortress which enemies cannot destroy.

An ancient India was an advanced knowledge society. Invasions and colonial rule destroyed its institutions and robbed it of its core competence. Its people have been systematically degraded to lower levels of existence. By the time the British left, our youth had lowered their aims and were satisfied earning an ordinary livelihood.

India is essentially a land of knowledge and it must rediscover itself in this aspect. Once this rediscovery is done, it will not require much struggle to achieve the quality of life, strength and sovereignty of a developed nation.

Knowledge has many forms and it is available at many places. It is acquired through education, information, intelligence and experience. It is available in academic institutions, with teachers, in libraries and in research papers. Knowledge is available in seminar proceedings and in various organizations and workplaces with workers, managers, in drawings, in progress sheets and on the shop floors. Knowledge, though closely linked to education, comes equally from learning skills such as those possessed by our artists, craftsmen, hakims, vaidyas, philosophers and saints as also our housewives. Knowledge pays a very important role in their performance and output.

Our heritage and history, the rituals, epics and traditions that form part of our consciousness are also vast resources of knowledge as are our libraries and universities. There is an abundance of unorthodox, earthly wisdom in our villages. There are hidden treasures of knowledge in our environment, in the oceans, bio-rivers and deserts, in the plant and animal life. Every state in our country has a unique core competence for a knowledge society.

Knowledge has always been the prime mover of prosperity and power. The acquisition of knowledge has, therefore, been the thrust area throughout the world.

The knowledge society has very important components driven by societal transformation and wealth generation. The societal transformation is in respect of education, healthcare, agriculture and governance. This will lead to employment generation, high productivity and rural prosperity.

The task of wealth generation for the nation has to be woven around national competencies. We have identified core areas that will spearhead our march towards becoming a knowledge society. The areas are- information technology, biotechnology, space technology, weather forecasting, disaster management, telemedicine, tele-education, technologies utilizing traditional knowledge and service sector. Infotainment is one more important area which has emerged resulting from convergence of information and entertainment. These core technologies, fortunately, can be interwoven by IT, a sector that took off only due to the enterprising spirit of the young. Thus, there are multiple technologies and appropriate management structures that have to work together to generate a knowledge society.

Rural development is an essential need for transforming India into a knowledge superpower. And high bandwidth rural connectivity is the minimum requirement to take education and health care to the rural areas.

Maharshi Patanjali says in the Yogasutra, "When you are inspired by some great purpose; by some extraordinary projects, all your thoughts break their bounds. Your mind transcends limitation. Your consciousness expands in every direction, and you find yourself in a new, great and wonderful world. Dormant forces, faculties, and talents become alive. You discover yourself to be a greater person by far than you ever dreamt yourself to be."

It is the people of a nation who make it great. By their efforts, the people in turn become important citizens of their great country. Ignited minds are the most powerful resources on the earth. One billion minds of our nation are indeed a great power waiting to be trapped.

Ancient India was a knowledge society that constituted a great deal to civilization. We need to discover that status and become a knowledge power. We must learn from our mistakes to achieve a better standard of life. A developed India will supplant a spirit of defeat with the spirit of victory.

GETTING THE FORCES TOGETHER

Determine that things can and shall be done, and then we shall find the way. —Abraham Lincoln

Progress is rapid wherever there is an efficient administrative set-up. Progress is rapid wherever there is a high level of education and minimum political interference in development activity. To Dr. Kalam, development is a security—a centric phenomenon—from poverty to food security, social security and, therefore, national security.

In "India Vision 2020", Dr. Kalam says: "We have identified five areas where India has a core competence for integrated actions:

Five among these, one is agriculture and food processing where we have to set a target of three hundred and sixty million tonnes of food and agricultural production. Agriculture and agro food processing, particularly by way of value addition, would bring prosperity to the rural people and speed up economic growth.

The second area is power. A reliable supply of electricity in all parts of the country is a must.

The third area is education and healthcare. Here we have found that education and healthcare are inter-related. For example, Kerala with high literacy and better healthcare could bring down the rate of population growth and made more improvements in the quality of life in the state.

The fourth area is information technology. This is one of our core competencies and holds the potential to rapidly transform backward areas, besides promoting education and generating wealth.

The fifth sector is the strategic sector. This area, fortunately, has witnessed growth in areas like nuclear, space and defence technology."

Action in these five areas, properly integrated, would lead to food, economic, social and national security. A strong partnership between the research and development institutions, universities, industries and the community as a whole with the government departments and agencies will be essential to accomplish the vision. The key to success lies in connectivity.

The development of education and healthcare will yield the benefits of smaller families and a more efficient workforce. It is the key to employability and social development. Improvement in the agriculture sectors, including that of food processing, would lead to food security, employment opportunities and rapid economic growth. Growth in the information technology sector would assist rapid economic growth as well as play an important part in speeding up development. Electric power provides energy security so crucial for all sectors. The strategic sector has a direct impact on industry, sustaining growth and technological strength. For balanced developments, all the five areas are of importance. The combined effect of these five areas would result in GDP growth of our country and the betterment of lives of millions of our countrymen who are presently living below the poverty line.

The vision of a developed India can be realized only if we recognize that wealth generation and wealth protection are two sides of the same coin. A nation's wealth represents the sweat and hard work of its people.

Another aspect of a developed country is global competitiveness of its industry. It is not only catering to the home market but also aiming for a large market outside it. Hence, its contribution to GDP is also very large. Indian industry has to show the same competitiveness and innovation so that we can have our own multi-nationals.

Universal literacy and access to education for all is another fundamental requirement for a nation to be truly developed. Education would result on the creation of a large base of people who excel in various fields as well, an invaluable resource for any country.

World competitiveness is a combination of the progressiveness of industry, the push of improved technology and the status of governmental deregulation.

We need to adapt the implementation of our programmes. We need to adapt the policies into a mission mode to succeed. Progress cannot be swift and far reaching, if the path is full of potholes. The abundant national resources—human and material remain to be fully unutilized.

BUILDING A NEW STATE

If I were to look over the whole world to find out the country most richly endowed with all the wealth, power and beauty that nature can bestow—in some parts a very paradise on the earth—I should point to India. —F. Max Muller

The way to development is through purposeful activity. The young especially have to be guided properly, so that their lives find a proper direction and their creativity is allowed to flower. To facilitate this, certain educational reforms must be initiated.

With regard to improving the pace of development, centre-state efforts should be co-ordinated in a few key areas. Efforts across sectors and organizations should be integrated and taken up in a mission mode. The mind-set must change showing willingness to take pragmatic risks. Success will follow.

13

TO MY COUNTRYMEN

Where the mind is without fear and the head is held high;

Where knowledge is free;

Where the world has not been broken up into fragments...

My Father, let my country awake.

—Rabindranath Tagore

Students should get ready to transform India into a developed nation. Ignite your minds and think big.

We must be aware of our higher Self and view ourselves as citizens of a developed nation. We are a great civilization and each one of us born here must trust in the wisdom of his civilization. Our scriptures tell us that there is no barrier between us and the world. They tell us that we are the world just as the world is in us. It is for you to put yourself in tune with the music of the universe.

We want all of us—institutions, political parties, industries, communities, families, individuals-at every level to take full responsibility to what is good or bad in our situation, for what we possess and that which we do not. This would mean that we stop blaming others for the circumstances we find ourselves in. Taking responsibility also means a willingness to exercise our abilities to the fullest. This will make us worthy of enjoying the benefits that come with effort.

The needs of a nation's people are bigger and more important than any other considerations. The mission of parliament is that it has to be alive and dynamic over issues vital to the existence of our very nationhood. Your freedom did not come as a gift. The whole country struggled for decades to achieve the first vision of indepedence. So, we have to protect it. There were excellent leaders in all walks of life-science, education and industry. To preserve this freedom from intruders and others who would compromise, it is our bounden duty and not a matter of choice and convenience. No ideology is above the security and prosperity of our country. No agenda is more important than harmony among the people.

The administrators have a great opportunity to link the people and political leaders. They should always take decisions that are good for the people. We believe it is only executives—empowered District Collectors who can assist transformation. The State Central integrated fund has to be deployed in mission mode programmes.

The results of scientific effort have not reached he people to the extent required. It is time the advances in science and technology are deployed in a big way to transform rural life.

Global competition is on. For industrialists, competing with high performance and cost-effective products win result in growth for the industry. Competitiveness and innovation are the two pillars of industrial growth. Industries by working together can generate multinational institutions reversing the present trend.

The IT community by its innovativeness has given India stature in the world. India is a competitive nation in IT today. Information Technology must be used for healthcare, telemedicine, to remove illiteracy, to generate skills, and for e-governance and tele-education. Transform the nation into a knowledge society with IT as the linking tool.

The farmers have given this country surplus food with their sweat. Time has come for two events to take place in agricultural sector. One is the value addition of all agriculture products. The second is to improve the quality of agriculture products and compare in the world market. Above all, marketing itself is a great business tool. We have to create a new centre for this purpose. These steps will bring relief to the farmers.

And to God the Almighty! Make our people sweat. Let their toil create many more *Agnis* that can annihilate evil. Let our country prosper in peace. Let any people live in harmony.

14
SONG OF THE YOUTH

Me and My Nation—India

As a young citizen of India,

Armed with technology, knowledge and love for my nation, I realize, small aim is a crime.

I will work and sweat for a great vision,

the vision of transforming India into a developed nation powered by economic strength with value system.

I am one of the citizens of a billion,

only the vision will ignite the billion souls.

It has entered into me,

the ignited soul compared to any resource,

is the most powerful resource,

on the earth, above the earth and under the earth.

I will keep the lamp of knowledge burning

to achieve the vision- Developed India.

15
ELECTIONS AND THE VOTERS

The below mentioned is the learning of Dr. APJ Abdul Kalam in respect of political reforms extracted from his popular book—"Governance for Growth in India" to be read and followed by every youth and political leader:

Always vote for the right kind of person. Casting no vote is no solution to any problem. You have to choose the best candidate based on their work and contribution to society. Many a time, the contribution is visible in the constituency from where they are contesting. There is also a record of their overall performance in the parliament assembly. Information on their performance is also available through the media and the internet. Based on the candidates' credentials, you can discuss among yourselves and select the best performing and cleanest candidate and vote for that person.

Remember, your right to vote is precious and to exercise your franchise is essential to have a great opportunity to select the right person to represent you in the Parliament or in the Assembly. This means, you as a young citizen, are helping the nation to evolve a good government at the Centre or State. The nation will be grateful to you, if you cast your vote and choose the right candidate.

Youth are an integrated and vibrant part of the democratic process. The youth of India want to see elected members as their role models through their performance in the Parliament or State Assembly, and also in the way they lead their lives.

They definitely expect the elected representatives to ensure that the performance of the Parliament and State Assemblies are never disturbed or halted. For them, the action of non-performance is a crime. Above all, the youth of the nation want their representatives to follow the mission of developmental politics. While choosing your candidate, ask him some questions:

1. What changes would you bring in your constituency after 2-5 years and after 5 years?

2. Do you have plans to realize 100 per cent literacy in your constituency? If so, you may indicate your plan.

3. With what skill and expertise will you empower the members of your constituency to increase the per capita income by at least two times?

4. Do you have a plan to plant at least 100,000 trees in your constituency?

5. How will you rejuvenate the water bodies in your constituency and activate their inlet and outlet?

6. How will you facilitate sanitary facilities in your constituencies with adequate water supply and its management?

7. Will you plan for multi-cropping and also for the plantation of Jatropha in the wasteland in your constituency?

8. How will you make your constituency free from power cuts and power shortage by using renewable energy sources?

9. Will you pave the way for peaceful and prosperous livelihoods of the citizens in your constituency?

16

OATH OF LEGISLATORS

1. I am proud to be a member of the Legislative Assembly/ Council of high tradition.

1. The welfare and happiness of the citizens of my constituency come first always and every time.

1. I will work hard to make the constituency fully literate, healthy, empowered and poverty free.

1. I will not allow any discrimination in my constituency by way of religion, language caste or creed.

1. I will be transparent in all my actions and become a role model for all the citizens of my constituency.

1. I will celebrate the success of the citizens of my constituency.

1. My constituency is my life and my state and the nation is my soul.

1. I will work with integrity and succeed with integrity.

17

THE TWO-PARTY SYSTEM

Dr. Kalam suggests the honourable members of the parliament like this:

India has to eventually graduate to a two-party system. There shall be two strictly defined coalitions with pre-poll affiliations and a clear-cut development agenda agreed upon by all the partners and publically debated over the electronic media.

We are witnessing an election in one or other parts of the country every now and then. There is a need for concurrent elections for State Assemblies and the Lok Sabha to minimize the time and resources spent on elections and provide time to the representatives for the development of the constituencies in a coordinated way.

We can evolve an election system which will bring about a stable government and which can fulfil the aspirations of the people and take the nation towards development.

We also have to study and analyse the various forms of democratic election system such as proportional representation so that people are enthused to participate in a big way to elect their representatives and recall their representatives when they don't perform.

SIMPLIFYING THE VOTING SYSTEM

We see rapid progress of information technology and communication infrastructure in the nation. It is time we look at how technology can be coupled with secure systems to simplify the voting process with the introduction of a unique identification number for each citizen. The Election Commission can consider the possibility of creating a system for internet or mobile based voting which is foolproof and devoid of any loopholes.

This technology interface will not only save costs but also enable large participation and promote safety, secrecy, and transparency. The same technology can be used to facilitate easier access to information about the candidates and their profiles using system such as emails, IVRS

(Interactive Voice Response System) based platform or through SMS (Short Messaging Service), MMS (Multi Media Service) as well as social media.

18

ROLE OF MEMBERS OF PARLIAMENT

The Parliament is a pivotal institution of democracy. But it has to revitalize itself in order to become a vibrant and progressive fortress of democracy. The parliamentarians' role assumes tremendous significance and it is essential that Members of Parliament live up to the aspirations and ideals for which they have been elected.

Our polling processes have been, sometimes, under severe strain with certain fatal incidents. Many a times, it creates doubts about our democratic system in the public eye. When politics degrade itself to political adventurism, the nation is put on the calamitous road to inevitable disaster and ruination. Let us not risk it. It is time for all of us to introspect and live up to the expectations that were enshrined so diligently and optimistically in our Constitution so that India may sustain itself and grow as a mature, healthy, vibrant and democratic nation.

The Parliament needs to mount a mission to identify and scrap the complete old laws and administrative procedure which are hindering a growth-oriented economy. This will give hope to a large section of people. The people need to develop more trust in their leaders and only the Members of Parliament can bring about this change.

Let us show to ourselves and the world the maturity we have gained in our politics and how we can utilize that is vibrant, vigilant, safe and secular. This is well within our capability and we can achieve it if we really strive towards it.

19

HOW TO ACHIEVE OUR POTENTIAL

If we do not talk differently, we shall not think differently. —TONY JUDT

History has proven that those who dare to imagine the impossible are the ones who break all human limitations. In every field of human endeavour, whether science, medicine, sports, arts, or technology, the names of the people who imagined the impossible and achieved greatness are engraved in our history. By breaking limits of their imagination, they change the world.

The challenge in our society from home to school and workplace is that we need visionary leaders at every level who have the capability to inspire others. We need to bring out the best in our youth and for this a leader has to be a good teacher. We are sure that the creativity and dedication of our youth will emerge by the integrated efforts of parents, teachers and leaders in all walks of life. Dr. Kalam gives us a message like this:

The seeds of the banyan tree are indeed like the citizens of the nation. Democracy and good governance are the power to provide equal opportunity to every citizen to grow and to perform, to become trees of their own. Every citizen, therefore, has the capacity to contribute to the vision of the country in his or her own way. Let us nurture every seed. Nevertheless, seeds that become manure must not be treated any lesser than the seeds that become trees.

How can you achieve your ambitions and unlock your potential? There are four proven steps:

1. Having an aim in life before you are twenty years of age.
2. Acquiring knowledge continuously.
3. Working hard with the aim to defeat any problem and to succeed, no matter what?
4. Having enough will-power and confidence to achieve great deeds.

My message to young friends is that education gives you the wings to fly. Achievement comes when your conscious and sub-conscious mind believes: "I will win."

Each one of you must have "Wings of Fire." The wings will lead you to knowledge which will, in turn, make you fly high as a doctor, an engineer, a scientist, a teacher, a political leader, a bureaucrat, a diplomat or anything else you want to be.

In our home or place of work, or in a park, we can plant ten trees and nurture them. You have to realize that every mature tree gives 14 kg of oxygen in a year and absorbs 20 kg of carbon dioxide through the process of photosynthesis. Thus, we can assist in creating a beautiful and pollution free environment.

20

THE INDIA WE VISUALIZE

We visualize a nation like this:

A nation where the rural and urban divide have reduced to a thin line,

A nation where there is equitable distribution and adequate access to energy and water,

A nation where the agriculture, industry or service sector work together in symphony,

A nation where education is not denied to any meritorious candidate because of societal or economic discrimination,

A nation which is the best destination for talented scholars, scientists and investors,

A nation where the best of health care is available to all,

A nation where government is responsive, transparent and corruption free,

A nation where poverty has been totally eradicated, illiteracy removed and crimes against women and children are absent and none in the society feels alienated,

A nation that is prosperous, healthy, secured, devoid of terrorism, peaceful and happy, and continues as a sustainable growth path, and

A nation that is one of the best places in the word to live in and one that is proud of its leadership.

Dr. Kalam suggests that each of us should select an important topic pertaining to any of the ten pillars which he has described based on one's interests and core competence and work towards realizing some part of this vision.

Our mission is to transform India into a developed nation and achieve the distinctive profile of India. There are five areas where India needs core competence:

1. Agriculture and food processing,
2. Education and healthcare,

3. Information and communication technology,
4. Infrastructure reliable and quality electric power surface transport, and
5. Self-reliance in critical technologies.

These five areas are closely inter-related. And progress in these areas in a coordinated way will lead to self-sufficiency in food, economic stability and the security of our nation.

For this to be a reality, the youth have to focus on inclusive governance.

21
OATH FOR THE YOUTH

Dr. Kalam has written the oath for the youth of India like this:

I will have a goal and work hard to achieve that goal. I realize that thinking small is a crime. I will work with integrity and succeed with integrity.

I will be a good member of my family, a good member of the society, a good member of the nation and a good member of the world.

I will always try to better someone's life without any discrimination on caste, creed, language, religion or state.

I will always protect and enhance the dignity of every human life without any bias. I will always work for a clean planet and for clean energy.

As a youth of my nation, I will work with courage to achieve success in all my tasks and enjoy the success of others.

I am as young as my faith and as old as my doubt. Hence, I will light the lamp of faith in any heart.

My national flag flies in my heart and I will bring glory to my nation.

22
TRAITS OF A GOOD LEADER

Characteristics of a good leader in the eye of Dr. Kalam follow as such:

1. A leader should be ready to give to others rather than expect others to give.
2. A leader should be equipped to manage change.
3. A leader should have nobility of heart.
4. A leader should have vision and clear thinking and the capability to be a facilitator.
5. A true leader needs to be passionate.
6. A true leader needs to travel on uncharted territory.
7. A true leader needs to have the courage to take quick and effective decisions.

Dr. Kalam teaches us that:

1. A leader must have a vision.
2. A leader must have the passion to realize the vision.
3. A leader must be able to travel on an unexplored path.
4. A leader must know how to manage both success and failure.
5. A leader must have the courage to take decisions.
6. A leader should have nobility in management.
7. A leader should have ability in management.
8. A leader should be transparent in every action.
9. A leader must work with integrity and succeed with integrity.

RULE OF LAW

Leaders have to regulate themselves by code of behaviour as ordained by the Constitution. Freedom available to them is to be used for the formulation of wholesome legalistic stipulations within the framework of the Constitution for common good. Discreetness is a virtue to be cultivated and exercised. Actions once taken cannot be undone.

Independence of jurisdiction does not mean license to override good senses. There is a denial of the rule of law, implicitly yet unmistakably, promised to the citizens by the Constitution of India.

Privileges are meant to be enjoyed with production by those on whom they are conferred. They are not meant to make others suffer. They are not certainly meant to be flaunted.

Rights are meant to be exercised for achieving the right thing. They are not to be brandished. Politeness and moderation are virtues to be cultivated by each of the organs of the system coupled with respect for others. They shall be consciously remembered and conscientiously followed with unflinching loyalty, sincerity and honesty.

Indian democracy faces many challenges, but we need to see these challenges as great opportunity.

23

NATIONAL DEVELOPMENT AND CREATIVE LEADERSHIP

A creative leadership can bring about national development. There is a certain connection between creative leadership and national development. Connections are like this:

A nation's economic development is powered by competitiveness.

Competitiveness is powered by knowledge.

Knowledge is powered by technology and innovation.

Technological innovations are powered by resource investment.

Resource investment is powered by return on investment.

Return on investment is powered by revenue.

Revenue is powered by volume and repeat sales.

Volume and repeat sales are powered by customer loyalty.

Customer loyalty is powered by quality and value of products.

Quality and value of products are powered by employee productivity and innovation.

Employee productivity is powered by employee loyalty.

Employee loyalty is powered by employee satisfaction.

Employee satisfaction is powered by the working environment.

Working environment is powered by management innovation, and

Management innovation is powered by creative leadership.

For success in all national missions, it is essential to have creative leaders. Creative leadership involves exercising the vision to change the traditional role from the commando to the coach, from manager to mentor, from director to delegator and from one who demands respect to one who facilitates self-respect. For enhancing enterprise value, we need a large number of creative leaders.

GOOD GOVERNANCE FOR INCLUSIVE GROWTH

Right to aspire for dignity and distinction is the prerogative of every citizen in a democracy. And for a successful democracy, good governance is needed.

We are a country of diversity. We have some of the richest people in the world on one hand, and millions of people living below the poverty line on the other. The core competence of a nation is its ability to manage a multi-lingual, multi-religious and multi-cultural society.

So the priority of our country should be inclusive growth and how to bring it about. For realizing this, we have to strengthen the multiple organs of governance. Our legislature, our executive, our judiciary and our media should be transformed.

THE INDIA WE ASPIRE FOR

Dr. Kalam visualizes India by the 2020 like this:

We have to create a nation where the rural and urban divide is minimal,

where there is equitable distribution of natural resources,

where various sectors of the economy show consistent growth,

where value based education is available to all,

where learned people receive recognition,

where healthcare is available to all,

where poverty is eradicated,
where governance is without corruption,

where woman receive equal opportunities in every stage of
life, and finally

we have to create a nation that is safe from strife.

INTEGRATED ACTION FOR DEVELOPED INDIA

To achieve this profile of India, we need to develop sectors like agriculture, education, healthcare, information & communication technology and infrastructure in all parts of the county in a coordinated and integrated manner. This can only be done through value based education and by building leadership at all levels. Leaders need to be educated. They need to be prepared for decision making, envisioning, planning and then implementing programmes. They also need to know how to manage failures.

24

CONFIDENCE IN GOVERNANCE

Good governance is being recognized as an important goal by countries across the world. Freedom of information is being redefined and supported by detailed guidelines. In this context, the internet revolution has proved to be a powerful tool for good governance initiatives. The internet enables the availability of services anytime anywhere a real possibility.

Along with this, there is also a conscious effort to put the citizen as the point of focus in governance. Citizens are being perceived as customers and the delivery of services to citizens is now being considered a primary function of the government.

As a function of governance, the government needs to provide multiple facilities and services to its people. These services also require to be constantly upgraded with the use of technology for fulfilling the changing needs and aspirations of the people.

The government is responsible for the betterment of the lives of the people by enacting appropriate policies and laws and by facilitating societal transformation. The success of the policies of government varies with the management style adopted by it.

THE CONCEPT OF E-GOVERNANCE

E-governance is a transparent and smart system of governance with seamless access. The authentic flow of information crosses inter-departmental barriers and provides fair and unbiased service to the citizens. Hence, we should use technology for the betterment of our society. E-governance is one such opportunity. Technology is a double edged sword. If we do not have an implementation plan from concept to completion, technology becomes expensive and we are not able to reap the benefits. Hence, it is essential for the nation to implement the e-governance process fast.

There is a knowledge grid. We have to transform an information society into a knowledge society. The knowledge society will be a society making and using products and services that are rich in both explicit and tacit knowledge.

RIGHT TO INFORMATION

The Right to Information Act has been in operation since 2005. A number of citizens have benefitted from seeking information on various aspects of the government. However, to derive maximum benefit from this Act, active participation of all stakeholders—political leaders, people in the civil services and the media, societal transformers and citizens is required. This will make India a highly participative democracy.

The country is poised to implement e-governance at all levels which, like the RTI, will bring further transparency in the process of governance.

EFFECTS OF CURRUPTION

Righteousness in the heart leads to order in the nation. In the absence of a non-transparent system, a well-intentioned programme fails to produce the desired result. This clearly shows the effect of corruption in governance and the failure of our system to protect the human rights of citizens. Levels of corruption vary from state to state. The reason for this should be established.

MISSION OF THE TEACHER

School is the next important environment where character is shaped. The prime learning period for children is between five to seventeenth years of age. School hours are the best time for learning. The school has the best of environment. As Bestolozzy, a Greek teacher said, "Give me a child of seven years. Afterwards, let the God or the devil take the child. They cannot change the child." That is the great confidence of the teacher. What a mission for teachers to build character and inculcate high morals in the student of the country!

ELEVATING YOUNG MINDS

Moral classes for students in order to elevate their minds are important. It is essential in secondary schools and colleges to arrange lectures by great teachers once a week on such a topic. This will elevate young minds and teach them to love the country, to love other human beings and inculcate noble values in them.

CORRUPTION FREE SOCIETY

A corruption free society is not merely a dream. It is entirely achievable. All we need is the role of enlightened citizens in the creation of a method of governance that promotes transparency and honesty for the better functioning of democracy.

Conscience is the light of soul. It raises its voice in protest whenever anything that is contrary to truth and righteousness is thought of or done. Conscience is a form of truth that has been transformed in the form of knowledge of our own acts. It knows right from wrong. Only a

virtuous and courageous person can use the instrument of consciousness
and that person alone can clearly hear the inner voice of the soul. In a
wicked person, that faculty is dead. The sensitive nature of the conscience
gets destroyed by sin or corruption and the person is unable to
discriminate right from wrong. Those who are leading organizations,
business enterprises, institutions and governments should develop this
virtue—the ability to use their own conscience.

Dr. Kalam recalls a hymn:

Where there is righteousness in the heart,

There is beauty in the character.

When there is beauty in the character,

There is harmony in the home.

When there is harmony in the home,

There is order in the nation.

When there is order in the nation,

There is peace in the world.

It reflects the beautiful connectivity between heart, character, home,
nation and the world. In a society, we need to build righteousness among
all its constituents. For the society as a whole to be righteous, we need
to inculcate values of righteousness in the family, in service, in career,
in business, in industry, in civil administration and in politics. We need
righteousness in law and order and in justice. When there is beauty in
heart, there is righteousness in character.

Electronic governance enables transparency which is needed for
corruption free society. If the corrective action is not done in real time,
the missile will not reach he target and the mission will be failure.
Guidance and control from its on-board computer act as the brain of the
missile. During the flying flight of the missile, computer is responsive for
guiding the missile to the target to meet the mission requirement and
success.

ENVIRONMENT

The environment can be cleaned up only through countrywide active participation of citizens. People as a team can participate in cleaning up the environment. Spiritual leaders can play a very important role in persuading devotees about the importance of the clean environment movement which, in turn, will promote the evolution of beautiful minds. Local groups can be formed to spread awareness about cleanliness in residential areas. Volunteers can proactively form these groups.

Industrialists should follow the prescribed norms for environmental standards in all their institutions. They should make buildings friendly to differently able people. Government employees should keep their offices and their environment clean. Parents and teachers should emphasize the need for environmentally friendly measures to younger citizens. Citizens can plant trees and nurture them in their neighbourhood every year. It is the responsibility of all stakeholders including the citizens to promote cleanliness in all these public facilities.

POLICE

While citizens demand that our police force has to be transparent and action-oriented, it is also essential that police stations are electronically connected. Simultaneously the police force needs to be empowered with quality of life like proper housing, sanitary facilities, medical cover and children's education. This will enable them to concentrate on their work with peace of mind and thereby the output from the police force would increase.

Dignity of women should be protected. They should get proper representation in all decision making institutions. Our panchayats truly represent the village citizens. They should ensure that all funds allotted for rural development in the areas are properly utilized for the intended purpose.

ARMED FORCES

Our armed forces and paramilitary forces are awake day and night guarding our borders on land, in air and at seas. They remain vigilant to counter a threat and facilitate unhindered progress of national development. Our police force, paramilitary and intelligence agencies complement each other to provide safety and security to our citizens from criminals and extremists. Many members of these forces have laid down their lives while protecting the people, the flag, and the nation. We salute them all.

COLLEGES AND UNIVERSITIES

Our colleges and universities must not only generate excellent entrepreneurs and researchers but also the best soldiers for our country. Parents should encourage the children to participate in national security mission. One must have the 'I can do it' spirit.

25

INDIA MUST HAVE A VISION

Many civilizations collapsed and many nations failed because they do not have the vision at the right time. The message here is that the youth want democracy to be re-invented with faster growth. The young mind is turbulent and looking for a vision for the nation and its fast accomplishment. It is very important to engage young minds with an inspiring vision for thinking and action.

National mission cannot be a part of a party agenda, but it can be a part of its election manifesto. It should be realized. The vision needs to be approved by the parliament so that there will remain continuity in its progress irrespective of the period of any government.

Hence, the elected leader of the nation should be a creative leader who walks the path of pursuing developmental politics adopting cooperation and collaboration as the key to operational procedure.

Dr. Kalam proposes the following action points for realizing our goal for an economically developed nation:

ENERGY

It is essential for the Indian parliament to ensure the Energy Independence Mission by 2030.Power generation through renewable energy has to be increased from 5 per cent to 28 per cent. Dependence on fossil fuels as primary energy source needs to be brought under 50 per cent from the present 75 per cent.

ENVIRONMENT

Enacting an inclusive environment enrichment policy is required. We need to increase the forest cover from 20 per cent to 40 per cent. We need to enrich the environment through mandatory zero liquid discharge and effluent discharge system for industrial waste. We need to encourage power generation from biomass and municipal waste at city corporations and village municipalities.

WATERWAYS

We need the implementation of the Smart Waterways Grid across India to harness 1500 BCM of floodwater. We need to connect the rivers and catchment areas as a single plane. The grid will receive 1500 BCM of floodwater and act as a water grid so that water can be released to any deficient place and replenished during flood. It would act as a 15,000 km national reservoir. It would be able to provide drinking water to 600 million people.

Apart from this, an integrated Water Resource Management Systems is also required to revive water bodies and tanks and build farm ponds and check dams across India as well as increase irrigation infrastructure and ground water potential, thereby enhancing the safe drinking water resources of the nation.

AGRICULTURE, MANUFACTURING AND SERVICE SECTOR

In agriculture sector, we need to launch the second Green Revolution Mission as an integrated agriculture, industry and service sector programmes with an air of 10 per cent growth rate in agriculture.

The manufacturing industry has to be empowered in order to achieve 25 per cent. It is essential to restructure viable industries with technology, business process and human resource. Proactive public policy is essential to relieve financial stress, to provide liquidity support and to save the productive assets of the country.

SCHOOL EDUCATION

Quality input generates quality output. The primary foundation for such action is the quality of teachers at the school level from the primary to the higher secondary level. The creation of a revamped National Quality Teacher Education System and its associated inclusive policy is essential. What we need is a creative syllabus, creative teacher and creative classroom for value-based quality school education.

HIGHER EDUCATION

The higher education system has to focus on research and development at the university level. Instead of monitoring and control by agencies such as UGC and AICTE, we should allow higher educational institutions to compete internationally by setting their educational standards at par with world class institutions so that they can be rated by independent agencies with a pool of eligible experts in the field on rotation. Minimum criteria may be set up for achieving excellence.

RESEARCH AND DEVELOPMENT IN HIGHER EDUCATION

Removing red-tapism and favouritism in higher education, research administration and management is of utmost importance. We need to empower universities—both government funded and private to promote research and enable them to improve research infrastructure. Establishing a National Research and Innovation Laboratory with access to all educational institutions at the state and central level is important. Incentives can also be provided to empower professors and students for research and development.

Good faculty attracts good research students. We need to attract a world class research faculty by creating a world class working environment, re-envisioning salary structures and providing accommodation in universities for possible collaborative international research projects. Universities should identify national challenges and direct their research towards finding innovative solutions. Every university should set up the centre for traditional research and development for local application for agriculture, industry and service sectors at the village level.

HEALTHCARE SERVICES

More medical colleges should be allowed to start provided they adopt government hospitals and invest in their infrastructure and health services and also adopt at least a hundred villages, PHCs, (Public Health Centres) in their neighbourhood. Medical teachers may also be imparted high definition tele-education technology by a well-qualified faculty and a medical laboratory. Practical applications may be tied up with government hospitals.

Comprehensible medical insurance provided by the government to unorganized sector needs to be introduced to provide quality healthcare services to the common man. Ensuring that quality healthcare reaches all states should be the prime objective of the nation.

INCLUSIVE GOVERNANCE

Inclusive governance means government that is responsive, transparent and corruption free. We need to achieve an 'Ease of Doing' business index. Introduction of e—governance with dynamic workflow management from top to bottom that connects the President, the Prime Minister, ministers, governors, CMO, state ministries, departments, secretariat, district collectors and ultimately the people is essential.

We also need to change in the Land, Mines and Minerals Act, internal security policy, inclusive industrial reforms, social justice and women reservation. We need to consider all other issues for redefinition with focus on inclusive growth with equitable social justice.

26

BRINGING PEACE AND PROSPERITY

India should not only work towards bringing sustainable peace and prosperity within its borders, but also among its neighbours. India is the second largest democratic nation in the word and its democratic values have been tested for more than seven decades.

If vision 2020 has to reap all the benefits of development, India has to see that all of its neighbours particularly the SAARC nations have attained peace and prosperity under democratic system. Otherwise cross border terrorism, naxalism and maoism will continue to threaten the very process of sustaining peace and prosperity. It is the responsibility of India to bring peace and prosperity to the subcontinent though democracy. Dr. Kalam suggests that SAARC nations work together in a way similar to the EU parliament which works towards promoting regional peace and prosperity.

UNITY OF MINDS

At this point, Dr. Kalam suggests that on a social level, it is necessary to work towards the unity of minds. Indian civilization is a multi-lingual, multi-faith, multi-racial system that has evolved over centuries. The increasing intolerance for the views and life styles of other and the expression of the intolerance through lawlessness cannot be justified under any context. All of us have to work hard to respect the rights of every individual. This is the most fundamental of all democratic values and our civilization—the very soul of our nation.

Let us evolve ourselves into a society that respects and celebrates differences. Let our experts, leaders and institutions show in their words and deeds:

Tolerance of other people's opinions.

Tolerance of other people's cultures.

Tolerance of other people's beliefs.

Tolerance of other people's styles.

Tolerance of other people's ideas.

In fact, such an attitude at the individual and community level has always been the hallmark of Indian civilization.

POLITICAL SYSTEM IN DEMOCRACY

Democracy works on the foundation of people's dreams and aspirations. It is not democracy that has to be reinvented. What needs to be reinvented is our political system with its responsibilities, its obligations and its boundaries.

WHAT WILL I BE REMEMBERED FOR?

Finally, I would like to ask every reader one question: What would you like to be remembered for? You have to evolve and shape your own life. You should write your goal down on a piece of paper. That page might just be a very important page in the book of a human history. And you will be remembered for creating that page in the history of the nation—whether that is a page of invention, of innovation, of discovery, of creating societal change, of removing poverty, of fighting injustice or execution of mission for energy independence.

Dr. Kalam gives us a message of courage. We need this courage to realize our dreams of happy, safe and prosperous nation:

Courage to think differently,

Courage to invent,

Courage to discover the impossible,

Courage to travel on an unexplored path,

Courage to share knowledge,

Courage to remove pain,

Courage to reach the unreached,

Courage to combat problems,

And succeed.

27
MOTIVATIONAL QUOTES OF
DR. APJ ABDUL KALAM

An inspiration to many, the 11th President, Dr. Avul Pakir Jainulabdeen Abdul Kalam is named as missile man for his contribution towards the development of India's missile projects. He often spoke to children and the country's youth inspiring them to think big in life. Here are some of his most inspiring and braining quotes:

Don't take rest after your first victory because if you fail in second, more lips are awaiting to say that your first victory was just luck.

Dream. Dream and dream. Dreams transform into thousands and thousands of results in action.

To succeed in your mission, you must have single minded devotion to your goal.

If you fail, never give up because fail means "First Attempt in Learning."

You have to dream before your dreams can come true.

Look at the sky. We are not alone. The whole universe is friendly to us and conspires only to give the best to those who dream and work.

You see, God helps only people who work hard. That principle is very clear.

The bird is powered by its own life and suits motivation.

Never stop fighting until you arrive at your destined place—that is You—the unique.

Have an aim in life. Continuously acquire knowledge. Work hard and have perseverance to realize the great life.

Teaching is a very noble profession that shapes the character, calibre and future of an individual. If the people remember me as a good teacher, that will be the big test honour for me.

Science is a beautiful gift for humanity.

If you want to shine like a sun, first burn like a sun.

You should not give up and we should not allow the problems to defeat us.

Creativity is seeing the same thing but thinking differently.

A man is great by deeds; not by birth.

Failures will never overtake me, if my determination to succeed is strong enough.

All of us do not have equal talents, but all of us have an equal opportunity to develop our talents.

All birds find shelter during the rain, but eagle avoids rain by flying above the clouds.

Man needs difficulties in life because they are necessary to enjoy the success.

Without your involvements, you cannot succeed. With your involvements, you can't fail.

Those who cannot work with their heart, achieve but a hollow. Half-hearted success breeds bitterness all around.

For great men, religion is a way of making friends. Small people make religion a fighting tool.

When learning is purposeful, creativity blossoms; when creation blossoms, thinking emanates; when thinking emanates, knowledge is fully lit and when knowledge is lit, economy flourishes.

Thinking is the capital enterprise in the way. Hard work is the solution.

Failure will never overtake me if my definition to succeed is strong enough.

Be active. Take on responsibility.

Work for the things you believe in. If you don't, you are surrendering your fate to others.

Great dreams of great dreamers are always transcended.

The most beautiful things in life are not things but people, memories and pictures. They are feelings, moments, smiles and laughter.

Old friends are Gold. New friends are Diamond. If you get a Diamond, don't forget the Gold because when you hold a Diamond in a ring, you always need a base of Gold.

Life is hard but not impossible.

Never stop learning because life never stops teaching.

Rejection is an opportunity for your selection.

Every new day is another chance to change your life.

Alphabet 'O' stands for 'Opportunity' which is absent in yesterday; available once in T 'O'day and thrice in T 'O'm 'O'rr 'O'w. Never lose hope.

Be patient. Sometimes you have to go through the worst to get to the best. Give you some time.

I don't know how my story will end, but nowhere in my text will it ever read... "I gave up."

Small steps in the right direction are better than big ones in the wrong direction.

The richest wealth is wisdom. The strongest weapon is patience. The best security is faith. The most effective tonic is laughter. And surprisingly, all are free.

Everything happens for a reason. That reason causes change. Sometimes it hurts. Sometimes it is hard. But in the end, it is for the best.

We always work for a better tomorrow. But when tomorrow comes, instead of enjoying, we again think of a better tomorrow! Let's have a better today.

A tree that wants to touch the sky must extend its roots into the earth. The more it wants to rise upwards, the more it has to grow downwards. So to rise in life, we must be humble, grateful and down to earth.

Remember that people will always question the good things they hear about you, and believe the bad ones without a second thought.

Do a one hundred things right. And someone will still point out the one thing you did wrong.

Positive thinking is not only about expecting the best to happen. But it is also about accepting whatever happens for the best.

In life, no one will remember how you looked, walked, talked or what you did. Everyone just remembers you by the way you made them feel when they were with you.

When we are wrong and we surrender, it means we are honest. When we are in doubt and we surrender, it means we are wise. But when we are right and we surrender, it means we value relations.

You are responsible for your happiness. If you expect others to make you happy, you will always be disappointed.

Being defeated is often a temporary condition; giving up is what makes it permanent. Never stop trying. Be positive. Think positive.

A door is much smaller compared to the house. A lock is much smaller compared to the door. A key is the smallest of all, but a key can open entire house. Thus, a small thoughtful solution can solve major problems.

Knowledge will give you power, but character will give you respect.

Patience is more than just having the ability to wait. It is about your attitude while you are waiting.

Our parents were patient when we were young. Now, it is our time to be patient during their old age.

Do the right thing even when no one is looking. It is called integrity.

If people say something bad about you, judge as if they know you. Don't feel bad. Just remember dogs bark if they don't know the person.

Mind and umbrella have one thing in common. They are useful when they are open, otherwise they increase our burden.

Life is not a music player to listen your favourite songs. It is a radio you must adjust yourself to every frequency and enjoy whatever comes in it.

The winners are those who learn to take full responsibility for their actions. The losers are those who blame others for their failures.

Expecting and accepting are two sides of life. Where expecting ends in tears, accepting makes you cheer. Accept your life the way it comes.

Good decisions come from experience. But experience comes from bad decisions. This is life. So don't worry for any mistake. Go ahead and learn from them.

Rumours are created by haters; spread by fools and accepted by idiots.

Never stop chasing your dreams. Life can take you from zero to hero in a fraction of time.

Your best teacher is your last mistake.

We cannot change the past, but we can start a new chapter with a happy ending.

Don't depend too much on anyone in this world because even your own shadow leaves you when you are in darkness.

Beauty attracts heart, but character attracts soul.

Whatever you do—good or bad, people will always have something negative to say.

Stop trying to change someone who doesn't want to change. Stop giving chances to someone who abuses your forgiveness. Stop trusting his words and ignore his actions. Stop walking back to the place where your heart ran from.

Stop breaking your own heart.

Sometimes saying sorry is the most difficult thing on the earth. But it is the cheapest thing to save the most expensive gift called relationships.

Umbrella can't stop the rain but can make us stand in rain. Confidence may not bring success but gives us power to face any challenge in life.

Wrong is wrong, even if everyone is doing it. Right is right, even if no one is doing it.

Success is when your signature changes to autograph.

If you fail, never give up because F.A.I.L. means "First Attempt in Learning."

End is not the end. In fact, E.N.D. means "Effort Never Dies."

If you get 'no' as an answer, remember N.O. means "Next Opportunity." So let's be positive.

Our best book is equal to one hundred good friends but one good friend is equal to a library. I am not handsome but I can give my hand to someone who needs help because beauty is required in heart not in face.

You cannot change your future. You can change your habits. And surely your habits will change your future.

Success is a journey, not a destination.

When writing the story of your life, don't let anyone else hold the pen.

The best brains of the nation may be found on the last benches of the classroom.

Sometimes it is better to bunk a class and enjoy with friends because now when I look back, marks never make me laugh, but memories do.

Death is not the greatest loss in life. The greatest loss is what dies inside us while we live.

Never ignore a person who loves you, cares for you, and misses you. Because one day you might wake up and realize that you lost the moon while counting the stars.

Honest relations are just like water—no colour, no shape; no space, no taste, but still the most important for life.

Very Nice Definition of Time:

Time is slow when you wait.

Time is fast when you are late.

Time is deadly when you are sad.

Time is short when you are happy.

Time is endless when you are in pain.

Time is long when you feel bored.

Every time, time is determined by yours feelings and your psychological conditions and not by clocks. So have a nice time always.

Theory of Life:

When flood comes, the fish eat ants. But when water dries, the ants eat fish. Life gives chance to everyone. Just have to wait for our turn.

Never judge a person you don't know his story.

Black colour is sentimentally bad, but black board makes the students' life bright.

A bird sitting on a tree is never afraid of the branch breaking because her trust is not on the branch but on its wings.

Work hard in silence; let your success be your noise.

Being positive does not mean ignoring the negative. Being positive means overcoming the negative.

Relations are life electric currents. Wrong connection will give you shocks throughout your life, but the right ones will light up your life.

Love your job but don't love your company because you may not know when your company stops loving you.

2 get and 2 give creates many problems. Just double it. 4 get and 4 give solves many problems.

A positive mind finds opportunity in everything. A negative mind finds fault in everything.

Life is like a book. Some chapters are sad; some happy and some exciting. But if you never turn the page, you will never know what the next chapter holds.

Sometimes you may not know the true value of a moment until it becomes a memory.

Your birth could have been an incident but your death should be history.

Twelve Things To Always Remember:

1. The past cannot be changed.
2. Opinions do not define your reality.
3. Everyone's journey is different.
4. Nearly all things get better with time.
5. Judgements are a confession of character.
6. Over thinking will lead to sadness.
7. Happiness is found within.
8. Positive thoughts create positive things.
9. Smiles are contagious.
10. Kindness is free.
11. You only fail, if you quit.
12. What goes around comes around.

Speak Five Lines To Yourself Every Morning:

1. I am the best.
2. I can do it.
3. God is always with me.
4. I am a winner.
5. Today is my day.

Never Forget Two People In Your Life:

1. The person who lost everything just to make you win (your father).

2. The person who was with you in every pain (your mother).

Though Dr. Kalam is no more now, he is still remembered by all of us for his notable contributions to India; for his presidency and also for his quotes which are inspiring the youth today. He wanted India to become a knowledge society. In a knowledge society, knowledge circulates through every individual. The individual needs not be a very learned man. He envisioned that even a housewife and a labourer will be a part of this knowledge society.

Dr. Kalam had a vision that India will become a knowledge superpower where people will live a comfortable life, where the nation would be able to defend her boundaries and where she will give her contribution for the humanity to progress. To make his dreams come true, all sections of the society would have to work on mission mode. If you are a scientist or an engineer, work hard with passion. Technological innovation is the only thing that can make our nation a military superpower. The USA and China are so proud of their military might! Pure scientific research is equally important because it pushes our technological boundaries. Everyone has his own role. Mind the following:

If you are a bureaucrat, work without and against corruption.

If you are a teacher, make students true patriots and unique thinkers and not mugging machines.

If you are a housewife, give your children more and more time.

As an Indian, respect your history and culture. Develop true knowledge and spread it without hesitation.

If each of us will do our job sincerely, the dreams of Dr. Kalam will come true.

If a country is to be corruption free and become a nation of beautiful minds, I strongly feel the three key societal members who can make a difference: They are the Father, the Mother and the Teacher.

My message, especially to young people, is to have courage to think differently, to have courage to invent and to travel on the unexplored path. The young people must have courage to discover the impossible and to conquer the problems. Let us sacrifice our today so that our children can have a better tomorrow.

Dr. Kalam further teaches us like this:

BE PREPARED

Life does not always follow the path we have set for it. Sometimes it takes its own move and makes us allow it instead. And when that happens in emergency, as some would term it, we better be prepared.

ROLE MODEL

He had always been an extraordinary individual. He incredibly served as the brilliant inspiration to many. Dr. Kalam was surely one such grand human being whose achievements, humility, sincerity, hard–work, positivity and never-give-up outlook would always impart a moral filling to all at every stage of life.

One of the most important characteristics of an ideal role model is "never to give up hope and hard work" in the face of oddities. One may be ready to throw challenges at different stages, but a true winner is he who does not get vulnerable to the unfavourable situation and keeps on finding always to beat the challenges and fight up to success. Dr. Kalam had been one such gallant fighter since his childhood. He always faces challenges with a smile.

Dr. Kalam was a great human being loved by all people irrespective of their social diversities. The whole nation mourned on his death on 27th July, 2015. Some principles that we must learn from him are:

HUMANITY

He respected all people equally even when he was the president. He used to listen to people's problem as a routine. He made regular interactions with students who he considered valuable assets of our nation.

RELIGIOUS TOLERANCE

He was unbiased throughout his life. He fought hard for nation's unity and maintaining secularism. Once when he was asked to ignite a lamp, he said, "Lamp is a holy thing in Hinduism and candle which you gave me to ignite is a holy thing in Christianity and I am a Muslim"—this is India.

HIGH GOAL IN LIFE

He always had high goals in his life and worked hard to achieve them. Once, someone asked him in an interview—"Why had he always goals in life?" He replied—"Life with goals is like a balloon with air as the balloon continuous to exist only if it has air." Not only he had great goals, but also he urged the students to have high ambition and work hard to achieve it.

We can learn about the principle and philosophy of high thinking-simple living. He was one who practiced it his whole life. No arrogance. No harsh behaviour but Strong vision and powerful implementation. Some questions as mentioned below can never be answered:

Can anybody hate the first rain after a famine?

Can anybody hate the wrath of sun after cold chilling day?

Can anybody hate a helping hand when you are really in trouble?

Can anybody hate a ray of hope when there are no chances left to overcome?

Can anybody hate a person who sacrificed his whole life for a nation and welfare of the society?

Can anybody hate a person who remained pure being on the highest chain of the country in this dirty world of politics?

Can anybody ignore a person who remained so humble in a world where showing off the things is the only matter of concern?

Can anybody deny Dr. Kalam?
The answer to all the above questions is 'No, no one'!

EPILOGUE

What Dr. Kalam wanted to tell the people of our country is that they must never be content with that which has been presented to them since our independence.

The full power of a banyan tree is equal to the power in the seeds of the tree. In a way both of us, you and me, are the same. But we exhibit our talents in different forms. A few of the seeds directly flourish as banyan trees and many seeds die.

Leaders must ensure that the younger generation is better than them. They must not subject the younger generations to circumstances that will stunt their growth. Above all, protection of the young from failures in scientific developments and constant encouragement is essential to ensure that scientists, technologists or those working in any field grow and work for the nation.

Apart from praying for the health and happiness of my teachers, friends

and relatives, I read this prayer:

O Almighty! Create thoughts and actions in the minds of the people of my nation so that they live united.

Help all religious leaders of my country. Give strength to all people to combat the forces of division.

Embed the thought "nation is bigger than the individual" in the minds of the leaders and people.

O God! Bless my people to work and transform the country into a prosperous nation soon.